OHIO
OHIO RIVER
COVINGTON
FRANKFORT
WEST VIRGINIA
LEXINGTON
RICHMOND
DANVILLE
VIRGINIA

To every librarian out there, fighting tirelessly to share books with children: You are my heroes! And to my sister, Amy. Thank you for cheering me on every step of the way. —L. H. K.

UNION SQUARE KIDS and the distinctive Union Square Kids logo are trademarks of Union Square & Co., LLC.

Union Square & Co., LLC, is a subsidiary of Sterling Publishing Co., Inc.

ISBN 978-1-4549-4848-3

Library of Congress Control Number: 2023053717

For information about custom editions, special sales, and premium purchases, please contact specialsales@unionsquareandco.com.

Printed in China

Lot #:

2 4 6 8 10 9 7 5 3 1

04/25

unionsquareandco.com

Interior and cover design by Marcie Lawrence

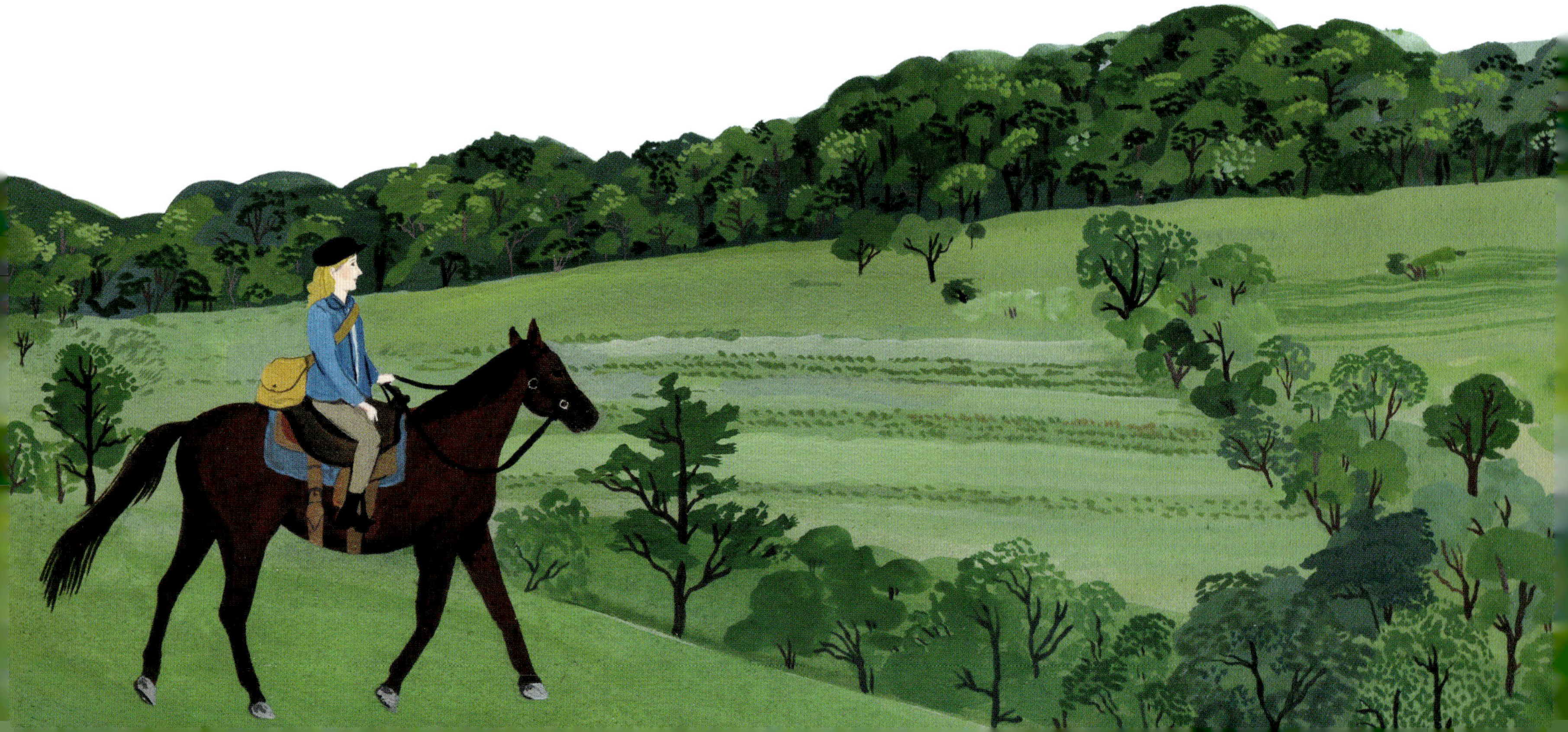

HOPE RODE

★ THE PROMISE OF THE PACKHORSE LIBRARIANS ★

words by Lauren H. Kerstein

art by Becca Stadtlander

From the ashes of the Great Depression rose a **NEW DEAL**, and a dream.

A vision of a new world **WHERE BOOKS TOUCHED LIVES EVERYWHERE**.

Where Packhorse librarians passed written words and recorded stories from person to person . . . to remember forever.

USA
PACK HORSE
LIBRARY
WPA

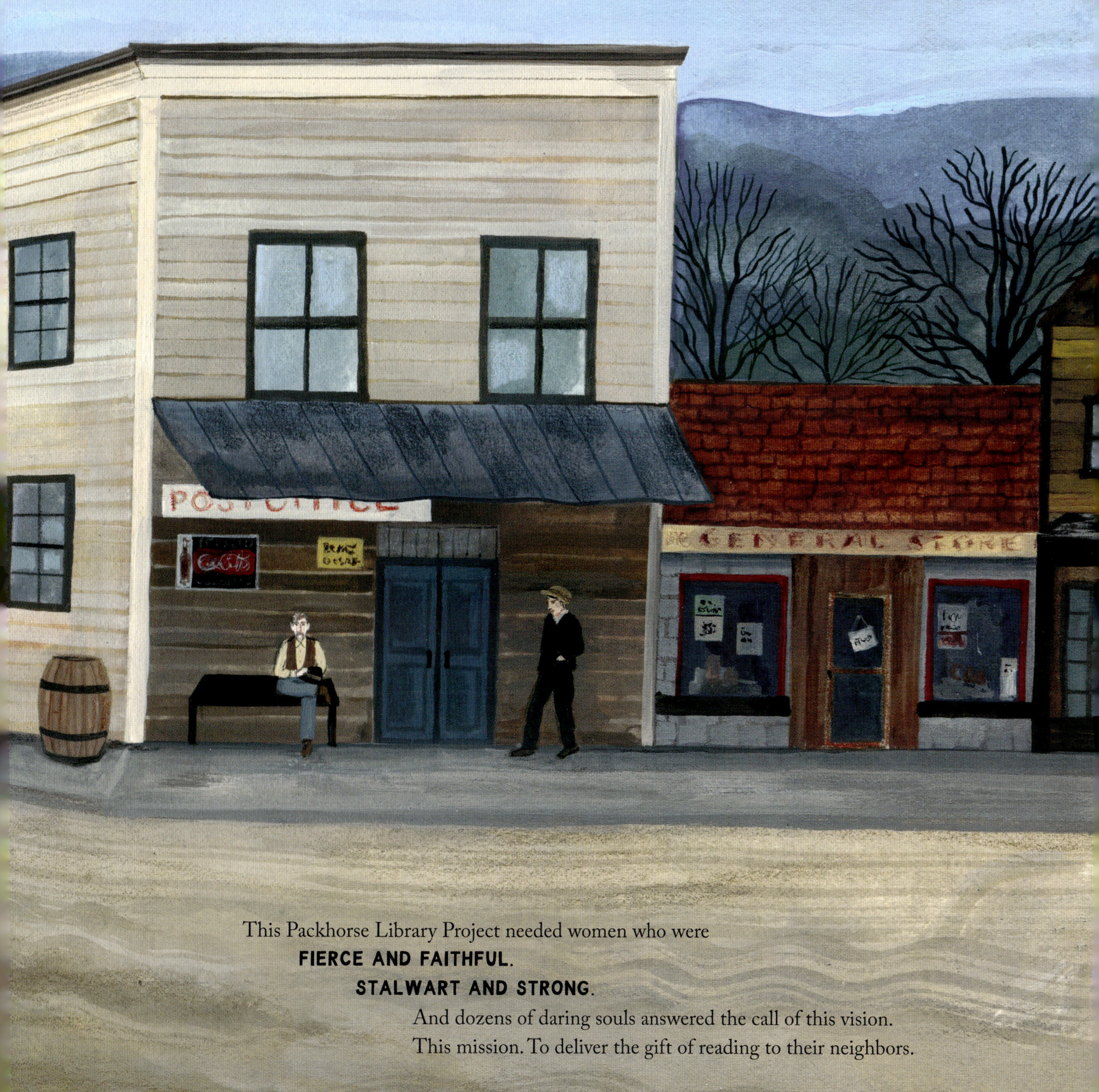

This Packhorse Library Project needed women who were

FIERCE AND FAITHFUL.

STALWART AND STRONG.

And dozens of daring souls answered the call of this vision. This mission. To deliver the gift of reading to their neighbors.

But even though the government hired librarians, they didn't provide supplies. So the librarians set to work.

CONNECTING,

COLLECTING,

AND CREATING.

They filled panniers, saddlebags, and pillowcases with books.

K GLUE
THE SECRET GARDEN
PRIDE AND PREJUDICE
DON QUIXOTE

They knew the road was treacherous.
That dangers lurked at every corner.

But this rural and remote land—the only home they'd ever known—needed books.

And so with friends by their side, they rode.

And as they strode, the sun's first rays kissed the Kentucky sky.
Dawn unfolded like a story waiting to be told.

A creek bed lay ahead.
A path where there was no other.

WATER SLOSHED.
ROCKS CRUNCHED.
DIRT SPRAYED.

Nature's music hummed,
welcoming and wondrous.

The promise of children's
smiles spurred them on.

The first stop appeared ahead.
Flush-cheeked children approached with curious eyes.

Laundry danced on the line.
Chipped wood creaked as the librarian stepped in.

"Learn me to read and then I won't be lonesome anymore," a child said. The librarian shared books the family had never seen.

SOFT WORDS.
NEW WORLDS.
A LIGHT IN DARK TIMES.

Stories smoothed frowns and eased pain.

And when it was time
to say goodbye . . .
a treasure for a treasure.

But the air felt damp, humid, and heavy.
A glance at the clouds proved rain was coming.

She prayed the worst of it would wait
until the day was done.

But it didn't.

Rain soaked her skin.
Slippery cliffs loomed ahead—

Rocks tumbled . . .
SPLASHED!

She listed left, barely steady.
Her bones sighed with weariness.
Hesitation hissed in her ears.

But a vision of excited smiles flashed in her mind.
She dug into her determination and—
jumped down.

It was safer to climb side by side. And stride by stride, they plodded on.
Through dark woods, thickening trees, bushes, and brambles.

Through leaves and rocks shifted by the storm.
Through mud and muck . . . to a cabin deep in the woods.

Librarians lived as neighbors, but they weren't always trusted.
For farms needed workers. Old *and* young.
And if books filled hands, hands weren't working.

Booted footsteps.

SNEERING.

LEERING.

FEARING.

Air as still as a puddle on a windless day.

Through dry mouth, thick throat, and trembling legs, the librarian pushed forward until—

she discovered a door in.

Visit after visit,
librarians wove books and stories into
the fabric of their neighbors' lives.

And as literacy **FLOURISHED**,
new ideas did too.

Though they might travel for hours without seeing another . . .
nature's hymns provided a constant companion.

WIND WHISTLED.
BIRDS SANG.
CREEKS BURBLED.

Hearts rose with each steadying beat.
The librarian packed up to go.

Her favorite stop lay ahead—

the **SCHOOLHOUSE**.

Children rushed over—
anticipation bubbling.

The librarian selected a few books, and every child crowded around for a read aloud.

Wide-eyed wonder blossomed as each page turned.

Quick questions.
Whispers of joy.
Bursts of laughter—
the sweetest sounds.

New dreams **DAWNED**.
Big ideas **FORMED**.
Seeds rooted and **GREW**.

With saddle settled—
Firmly fastened, up and in she
climbed . . . until next time.

Day after day, for nearly nine precious years . . .
These brazen, bold, and brave women rose to the call,

to a **VISION**,
to a **MISSION**–
deliver books to one and a half million patrons.

Families inhaled possibility and exhaled isolation as these fearless librarians taught children *and* adults how to read.

Although their journey wasn't a well-known chapter in Kentucky history, their impact changed the world forever.

The Packhorse librarians opened roads to knowledge, connection, and jobs.

They filled their neighbors' hearts, minds, and souls.

Though librarians faced
one hundred miles a week,
in winter's frost and summer's heat.

Though reins bit.
Feet froze.
And heat scorched.

Mile after mile . . .
Week after week . . .

HOPE RODE.

★★ Author's Note ★★

"THE PACKHORSE LIBRARY PROJECT WAS THE THING THAT REALLY GOT THE CHILDREN INTERESTED IN READING, AND GAVE THEM A DESIRE TO READ."
—Carrie Lynch, schoolteacher

Packhorse librarians in Hindman, KY.

Why start a Packhorse Library Project?

In 1936, the United States was experiencing the Great Depression. Jobs were hard to find. President Franklin D. Roosevelt created a federal program called the Works Progress Administration (WPA) to help, but most of the jobs were for men. First Lady Eleanor Roosevelt and Elizabeth Fullerton, Kentucky's state director of women's and professional projects, wanted to help women find jobs too. They also believed everyone needed to have access to books, so they started the Packhorse Library Project. The project drew inspiration from previous attempts by May Stafford (1913) and Berea College (late teens / early 1920s) to deliver books to rural areas. But each of these programs had ended by 1934, when the first Packhorse library began in Leslie County.

How would the Packhorse Library Project help?

Only 31 percent of people in Eastern Kentucky knew how to read, but learning to read could lead to better paying and safer jobs. Packhorse librarians taught people to read and connected them to the outside world, delivering books to families in rural and remote places who may not have been able to access books otherwise.

Eleanor Roosevelt visiting the Packhorse Library in West Liberty, KY.

Who were the Packhorse librarians?

By 1939, more than thirty women rode horses or mules (that they had to rent or borrow) over assigned trails to deliver books to schools and homes in the communities in which they lived. Roughly fourteen rural libraries had been established. Many women were married and raising children alone because their husbands had left to find work. It was up to the women to support themselves and their families.

"I RODE IN ALL TYPES OF WEATHER, PLOWING THROUGH KNEE-HIGH SNOW OR SLEETING RAIN THAT LEFT ICE CRYSTALS CLINGING TO MY COAT. ONCE, MY SHOES FROZE TO THE STIRRUPS."

—Grace Caudill Lucas

Children at a WPA library.

How did the program grow?

Teachers relied on Packhorse librarians for books and resources. Although some patrons were opposed at first, they grew to love the program, and requested more and more reading material. Word spread. Other counties began Packhorse Library Programs too.

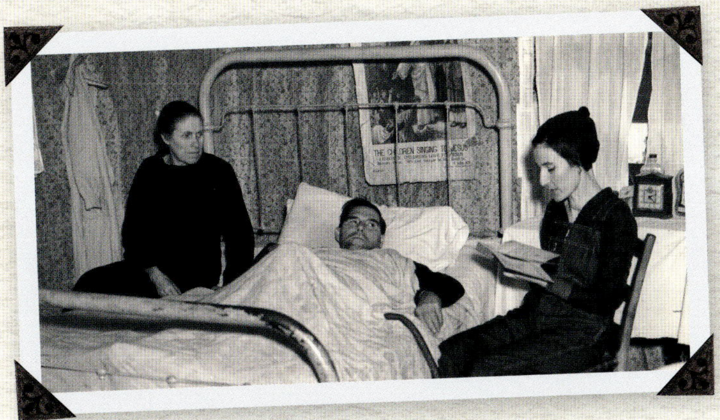

Librarians read to those who were injured or ill to provide comfort, companionship, and escape.

Library Programs in African American Communities

Although there is no evidence that the Packhorse Library Program was offered in BIPOC communities, library services were extremely important to African Americans. The following is a picture of a library in Frankfort, which was part of the WPA's Library Extension Program.

Library Extension Program in Frankfort, KY.

A Packhorse librarian at one of her regular stops.

Children enjoying story time.

How did the librarians gather materials?

They were not given materials as part of the program. Penny drives, donations, and community support helped the librarians collect reading materials. Once they collected books, newspapers, and magazines, they worked hard to protect them. Librarians created bookmarks out of greeting cards so that pages weren't "dog-eared" and destroyed. Librarians created 2,582 scrapbooks from bits and pieces of books and magazines that had become damaged beyond repair. They even added gifted recipes from patrons.

The Packhorse librarians also added text and commentary to the scrapbook pages. The scrapbooks were loved by all.

What impact did the Packhorse Library Project have?

The Packhorse Library Project helped thousands of families learn to read. This led to new skills, jobs, and hope during a dark time. In 1937, circulation had reached 60,000 books per month. Packhorse librarians visited 26,000 families and 155 public schools.

This powerful program even inspired Kentucky Representative Carl D. Perkins to request the first federal funding for public libraries. As a former one-room schoolhouse teacher, he'd received life-changing visits from Packhorse librarians.

With tenacity, courage, and compassion, Packhorse librarians changed lives one book at a time.

"THEM BOOKS YOU BROUGHT US HAS SAVED OUR LIVES."
—Packhorse recipient

"WE WERE SO HAPPY TO GET A BOOK. TICKLED TO DEATH. WE ALWAYS SAT UNDER THE BIG OLD CHESTNUT TREE. THEY DIDN'T KNOW HOW TO READ SO I READ IT AND READ IT AGAIN SO WE COULD UNDERSTAND IT."
—Mary Ruth Shuler Dieter

Dieter was one of the Packhorse librarians. She read to children and families until they were able to read to themselves.

The Packhorse librarians included recipes in their scrapbooks that were shared by families along their route.

★★ Bibliography ★★

A selected bibliography, additional reading/videos, and educational resources can be found at LaurenKerstein.net.

★★ Acknowledgments ★★

My Packhorse journey began with a book by Jojo Moyes called *The Giver of Stars*. I devoured the story from cover to cover, read and reread the postscript and acknowledgments, and listened intently when my critique partner, Katie Frawley, agreed with me that, "Yes! This should be a picture book." From there, I read *The Book Woman of Troublesome Creek* by Kim Michele Richardson, *Down Cut Shin Creek: The Pack Horse Librarians of Kentucky* by Kathi Appelt and Jeanne Cannella Schmitzer, and every other fiction and nonfiction book I found. I also conducted numerous interviews, which were both enlightening and fascinating. Whether I was reading fiction or nonfiction, book or article, or talking with an expert, my awe and admiration for these incredible women grew. I was determined to write a book that would do their work justice.

Although writing appears to be a solo activity, it isn't. I have so many people to thank who helped me along the way. Thank you to my incredible critique partners who read this book over and over and over again. I don't know where I'd be without you. A thank-you to Kathi Appelt, Jeff Urbin, Danielle Adams, Emily Jones Hudson, Jason Vance, Chelsea Brislin, Wyatt Woodson, Laken Brooks, Reinette F. Jones, Esther Cajahuaringa, Sally Hosokawa, Emily Duffy, Erin Dealey, and Deborah Warren. Without you, this book would not have been possible. And finally, thank you to Kim Michele Richardson and Jojo Moyes for writing incredible works of fiction that illuminated and expanded the lives of these steadfast and inspirational librarians.

I also want to acknowledge the challenges I faced ensuring I represented the BIPOC community accurately in this book. Despite extensive research, I was unable to find evidence that the Packhorse Library Project extended into communities of color. Schools and libraries were segregated during this time. As such, we made the extremely difficult decision to only include white librarians and patrons in the illustrations in order to be as historically accurate as possible. As noted earlier, the Library Extension Program, also established under the WPA, included outreach services to rural African American communities from main library offices that were located in towns. Berea College also offered library services. Reinette F. Jones explores this in her book *Library Service to African Americans in Kentucky: from the Reconstruction Era to the 1960s*, and was incredibly generous with her time as we talked this through by phone. I am also grateful to Emily Jones Hudson from the Southeast Kentucky African American Museum and Laken Brooks, folklorist, nonprofit educator, and researcher who pointed me in many helpful directions as I gathered as much information as possible.

And finally, thank you to Jason Vance for not only capturing so many incredible images of the Packhorse Library Program, but for sharing this rich history and these beautiful pictures with all of us.

INTERVIEWS CONDUCTED

Appelt, Kathi. Phone interview. May 11, 2022.
Brislin, Chelsea. Phone interview. May 25, 2022.
Brooks, Laken. Email interview. July 27, 2022. November 1, 2023.
Hudson, Emily Jones. Video interview. May 19, 2022.
Jones, Reinette F. Phone interview. November 7, 2023. Email interviews. November 2023.
Urbin, Jeff. Phone interview. May 13, 2022.
Vance, Jason. Video interview. May 16, 2022.

IMAGE CREDITS

Courtesy of Goodman-Paxton Photographic Collection, Packhorse Librarians in Kentucky WPA Project 1936-1943, University of Kentucky, Special Collections Library; Kentucky Department for Libraries and Archives; and Jason Vance.
Paper scraps: AKaiser/Shutterstock.com

KENTUCKY
N.
W
E
S
INDIANA
LOUISVILLE
ILLINOIS
OHIO RIVER
BARDSTOWN
MISSOURI
TENNESSEE